D0118656

New York
Enclaves

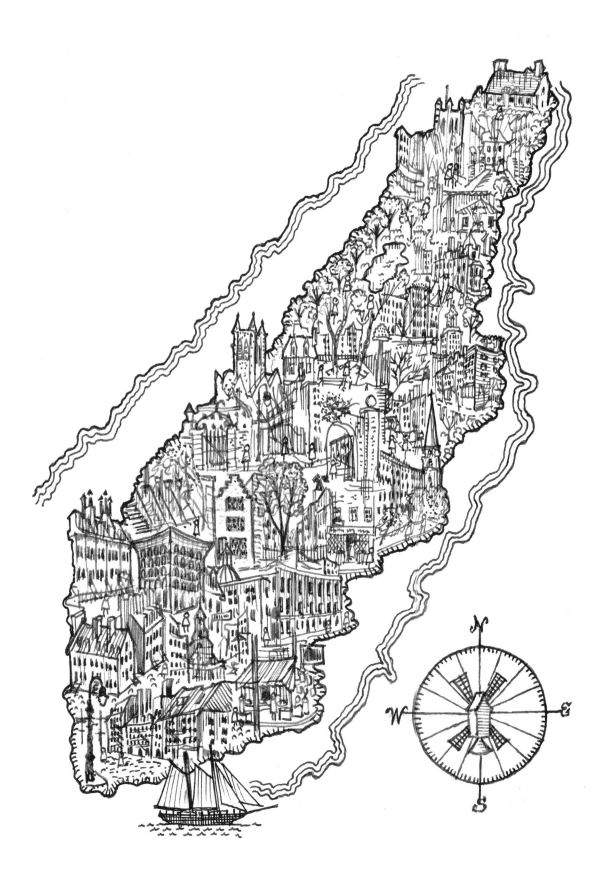

New York Enclaves

Written and Illustrated by
William H. Hemp

Clarkson Potter/Publishers
New York

Published by Clarkson Potter/Publishers, New York, New York. Member of the Crown Publishing Group, a division of Random House, Inc.

www.randomhouse.com

Originally published in slightly different form in 1975 by Clarkson Potter/Publishers, a division of Random House, Inc. CLARKSON N. POTTER is a trademark and POTTER and colophon are registered trademarks of Random House, Inc.

Printed in the United States of America

Design by Jan Derevjanik

Library of Congress Cataloging-in-Publication Data
Hemp, William H.
    New York Enclaves / William H. Hemp.
    Originally published: 1975.
    1. New York (N.Y.)— Description and travel.
    2. New York (N.Y.)—Pictorial works.   3. Streets—
New York (State)—New York.   4. Historic sites—New
York (State)—New York.   5. New York (N.Y.)—
History—Anecdotes.   I. Title.
F128.6.H45   2003
974.7'1—dc21   2002011008

ISBN 1-4000-4735-8

10 9 8 7 6 5 4 3 2 1

Revised Edition

For Maggie, again

On the Island of Manhate, and in its environs, there may well be four or five hundred men of different sects and nations; the Director General told me that there were men of eighteen different languages; they are scattered here and there on the river, above and below, as the beauty and convenience of the spot has invited each to settle. . . .
—FATHER ISAAC JOQUES,
FRENCH MISSIONARY

East Side, West Side, all around the town, the tots sang "Ring-a-rosie," "London Bridge is falling down," boys and girls together, me and Mamie O'Rorke, tripped the light fantastic on the sidewalks of New York.
—"THE SIDEWALKS OF NEW YORK,"
JAMES W. BLAKE, 1862–1935

Contents

Introduction

OVERSHADOWED BY SKYSCRAPERS, wedged between warehouses, hidden behind creaky iron gates, and tucked away like treasure chests in pirate coves, the enclaves of New York can be found: the alleys, cul-de-sacs, quiet courts, colorful marketplaces, nostalgic neighborhoods, secluded squares, storybook streets, and verdant parks that make up the mosaic of Manhattan Island today. Regrettably, few people stop to explore these pockets of brick and cobblestone or are even aware of their existence as they chatter into their cell phones while rushing along the sidewalks of New York.

This book, originally written and published in the 1970s, was the result of many hours of happy exploration; its purpose at the time was to call these places to the attention of townspeople and tourists alike. Now, with the dawn of the new millennium, the author has revisited these precious gems to see for himself how they have withstood the passage of time. While trees have grown taller, color schemes have changed somewhat, and next-door neighbors have moved away, most have met the test and survive today to transport the visitor to another time and place, to recall the talents of an icon, or to bring back memories of a dramatic episode in the history of Manhattan Island.

Webster's Dictionary defines an enclave as "a territorial or culturally distinct unit enclosed within foreign territory." Derived from the French verb *enclaver*, to enclose, there are dozens of places that fit this description between the Battery and Spuyten Duyvil, from the East River to the Hudson. A subway, bus, or taxi ride uptown, downtown, or crosstown can get you to almost any one in a matter of minutes. When you reach your destination, you suddenly find yourself in a foreign land. At some, you bask in the glow of lamplight from a bygone era. At others, you savor the atmosphere of an antique stage set far different from the modern-day metropolis.

What a story each enchanting enclave has to tell! Each is drenched in history, laced with the legend and lore of little old New York. The origin of one goes back to the days when Director General Peter Stuyvesant built a little chapel on his Bouwerie farm. Another, hibernating on Harlem Heights, served as George Washington's headquarters after a spirited battle in 1776. An area that was once a bustling seaport snuggles in the shadow of the Brooklyn Bridge. Other enclaves make up a chain of ethnic islands where immigrants from Ireland, Italy, Germany, the Caribbean, and China settled, making New York the greatest melting pot of peoples the world has ever known.

The twenty-six enclaves sketched in this volume form a multihued patchwork quilt ready to warm the hearts of city dwellers and out-of-towners alike:

Each characterizes a way of life that does not exist anywhere else; each has served as hearth and home for the potpourri of people who have made New York such a savory concoction; each holds a certain magic that over the past four hundred years has attracted merchants, mariners, and musicians, poets and politicians, actors and architects, butchers, bakers, and beer barons.

Once you've become acquainted with these New York enclaves, go and seek them out on your own. You'll discover that a trip to any one of these priceless mementos of the past is the best bargain to be found on Manhattan Island, that 9,800-acre parcel of real estate Peter Minuit, the second director general of New Amsterdam, purchased for the Dutch West India Company in 1626 from the Algonquin Native Americans with axes, trinkets, beads, and cloth valued at sixty guilders, or twenty-four dollars. Truly a Dutch treat!

South Street Seaport

WHITE-MANED WALT WHITMAN once described New York as the City of Ships, and South Street, in the early nineteenth century, was known as the street of ships. In those days the waterfront was a forest of masts, spars, and jibbooms. The bowsprits of clipper ships like the *Flying Cloud* stretched clear across the barnacled docks, poking their nautical noses almost into the windows of the ship chandlers' offices opposite. The street, lined with saloons like Jip and Jake's and Shanghai Brown's, swarmed with tattooed sailors, travelers, and townspeople scurrying to market. The odor of rum, molasses, wine, and spices was intoxicating.

You get a taste of the salty life on the old New York waterfront by setting course for the South Street Seaport. Here, a conglomeration of cobblestoned blocks, bounded by Peck Slip and Pearl, Front, John, and South Streets, has been restored in the heart of the old Fulton Fish Market, a flotsam and jetsam affair anchored along the East River.

On entering the seaport, you are welcomed by the *Titanic* Memorial Lighthouse, a monument to the 1,505 souls who died as heroes on April 15, 1912, in the North Atlantic collision with an iceberg of the White Star leviathan declared "unsinkable." At the foot of Fulton Street, beady-eyed gulls hover over a pilothouse that pipes you aboard the flotilla of tall ships and small boats floating proudly at the piers. These include the 1911 four-masted *Barque Peking;* the 1908 lobster-red *Ambrose Lightship;* the 1930 canary-yellow *W.O. Decker* tugboat; the fire-engine-red tugboat *Helen McAllister;* the 1885 schooner *Pioneer;* and the square-rigger *Wavertree,* launched in Scotland in 1885.

Just west of the wharf and Pier 17, a multi-tiered marketplace, stands Schermerhorn Row, a staggering sight of high-pitched roofs and Flemish bond brickwork. This business block was built during the War of 1812 by Peter Schermerhorn, a prominent citizen who ran a ship chandler's business on Water Street. It is the only remaining complex of commercial buildings in the Federal style of architecture in Manhattan.

The galleries of South Street Seaport Museum on Water Street contain a treasure trove of nautical memorabilia that includes the Der Scutt ocean-liner collection, Monarchs of the Seas. It showcases plans, models, and film footage evoking the majesty of a time when ocean liners like Cunard's RMS *Queen Mary* and the Art Deco SS *Normandie* were the last word in luxury travel.

Time to break for lunch and wet your whistle? Then land at the Bridge Café at 279 Water Street, housed in a sagging three-story red clapboard structure snuggling in the shadow of Roebling's masterpiece, the Brooklyn Bridge. The proud owners proclaim that it was originally listed as a wine and porter pub as early as 1794, making it Manhattan's oldest bar in the district's oldest remaining wood-frame building.

To landlubbers and seafarers alike, the South Street Seaport and the old Schermerhorn block tell the story of New York as a seaport city. By casting an eye about the timeworn cobblestoned streets and exploring the well-scrubbed ships, you are transported to 1524, when Giovanni da Verrazano, a Florentine in the service of Francis I, rounded Sandy Hook and sailed the *Dauphine* into New York Harbor, launching Manhattan Island's history as a haven for ships.

Washington-Harrison Street Houses

JUST A STONE'S THROW from the Hudson River and not very far from where the 110-story twin towers of the World Trade Center stood until tragically destroyed by a terrorist attack on September 11, 2001, huddles a small group of historic pink-brick dwellings known as the Washington-Harrison Street Houses. They make a touching tableau juxtaposed between two towering housing complexes on a cobblestoned street in the trendy district now known as TriBeCa (Triangle Below Canal).

These early Federal houses were not always anchored to this spot. Some were once situated two and a half blocks away amid the wagonloads of cabbages, cauliflowers, radishes, and rutabagas that once comprised the old Washington Street produce market. When that busy enterprise moved up to the Bronx, the federal government, under a special grant for historical restoration, provided the funds needed to relocate these houses to their present site at the corner of Greenwich and Harrison Streets.

The dwellings date from 1767 to 1828 and were built for specific owners on property that was originally part of the well-known farm of Annetje Jans. The land was granted to her by the director general, portly Wouten Van Twiller, in 1636. As the city grew up from Wall Street in the early nineteenth century, the commercial activities of the Washington Market expanded northward until, by the end of the century, the entire area was wholly commercial. By then there were no more than a handful of the original town houses left. Now that they have been grouped together and restored to their original glory in 1972–1974, the Washington-Harrison Street Houses present a late-eighteenth-century to early-nineteenth-century profile that exists nowhere else in the city of New York.

Who lived in this L-shaped cluster of charming dwellings during their early days? Well, we do know that the house situated at No. 31 Harrison Street was built in 1827 and originally owned by Jacob Ruckle. It is typical of the small but comfortable dwellings of the merchant class of New York City in the early nineteenth century. The dwellings at Nos. 29 and 33 Harrison belonged to Sarah R. Lambert and Ebenezer Miller, respectively. Nos. 315 and 317 Washington Street, now moved to Nos. 25 and 27 Harrison, were designed and built by John McComb, the city's first native-born architect. He also created New York's City Hall, completed in 1812 and considered to be the most beautiful in all fifty states. The McComb house at No. 27, with a fan-lit doorway, was the architect's own residence and one of the very few surviving Manhattan houses dating back to the eighteenth century—1796 to be exact. These houses once stood on what was once a very picturesque spot, beside a cove on a small spit of land, just one hundred feet from the river.

The Washington-Harrison Street Houses, with their high-pitch roofs punctuated by dormer windows and tall chimneys, show the craftsman-like attention to detail that is so characteristic of the Federal style. If John McComb were alive today, he would be content to know that the masterpiece in which he lived during his early years as an architect is now as sparkling fresh and spanking clean as it was back in 1796. That was during the days when the New York Stock Exchange was doing business beneath a grove of buttonwood trees in the open air on Wall Street.

Mott Street

When the fieldstone Church of the Transfiguration, at 25 Mott Street, was built in 1801, there was not a Chinese person to be found anywhere in New York. Then, in 1807, Pung-hua Wing Chong, John Jacob Astor's manservant, visited the city. Whether he was the first Chinese to settle on Manhattan Island is anybody's guess. Some say it was Quimbo Appo, who supposedly arrived in the 1840s. Others contend it was Ah Ken, a Cantonese merchant who opened a cigar store on Park Row. Whoever it was, he started Mott Street on the happy road to becoming the Main Street of New York's Chinatown, once called Five Points. With a population of about 150,000 residents, the enclave is now the largest Chinese community in the western hemisphere.

Today, Mott Street is as colorful as a dragon kite, as surprising as a fortune cookie, and home to the throngs of Chinese people scattered about the metropolitan area. It is to this cacophonous carnival below Canal Street and off Chatham Square, where chop suey was invented in 1896, that they come on weekends to shop, play mah-jongg, meet old friends, and dine in the exotic atmosphere of the ancient Orient.

One of the city's great adventures is a stroll down Mott Street at sundown amid the hodge-podge of tea parlors, restaurants, and souvenir stands. As you meander along, a peek into shop windows rewards you with mouthwatering displays of roast ducks with golden-brown skins.

The many-splendored treasure to be found on Mott Street is the rich collection of Chinese restaurants, some upstairs, some at street level, some subterranean. The fun comes in searching out a favorite for yourself. The cuisine is always authentic and prepared in one of many sumptuous styles, from the long-favored Cantonese to the more exotic Mandarin, spicy Szechuan, or hard-to-beat Hunan. Be it at a spotless lunch counter or in a lacquered emporium, you can feast on such favorites as scallops in black bean sauce or shredded beef beneath a warm blanket of snow peas.

Searching for a bit of antiquity? Well, you'll find it at 32 Mott Street General Store, the very oldest in Chinatown. This venerable emporium has been offering tea sets, brass Buddhas, jade statues, and decorative urns since 1891, when Lee Lok first opened its doors.

Strolling east off Mott to 13 Doyers Street, you arrive at the Nom Wah Tea Parlor, which is situated at the bend in the narrow lane. Since it opened in 1920, this tile-floored tea parlor has been a popular favorite with New Yorkers and visitors alike for its genuine Chinese tea luncheon. This usually consists of dim sum, an assortment of Oriental pastries such as minced pork with vegetables encased in a wonton covering, or ha gow, chopped shrimp with mixed Chinese vegetables encased inside a plump dumpling, served to your table from steaming carts on wheels.

For dessert, you might order a Frisbee-size almond cookie washed down with a scalding cup of oolong tea. Then queue up at the Chinatown Ice Cream Factory at 65 Bayard for a double scoop of green tea ice cream.

The Chinese New Year falls on the first full moon after January 21, and dancing dragons and serpentine chains of costumed children roll around the streets to the din of resounding gongs. But no matter what time of the year you make tracks to Mott Street, it is an unforgettable adventure and a gastronomical experience complete with chopsticks.

Orchard Street

REMEMBER THOSE SPIRITED SONGS by Irving Berlin? Those "'s-wonderful" Gershwin tunes? Those madcap Marx Brothers movies? Well, all these show-business greats had their roots in that neighborhood known as the Lower East Side, where Delancey Street ends at the Williamsburg Bridge.

The East Side story begins in 1880. That year New York had a population of about 80,000 Jews, mostly of German extraction. In 1881, Czar Alexander III began persecuting Russian Jews by forbidding them to acquire land and carrying out cruel pogroms. An exodus resulted, and by 1910 a total of 1.5 million Jews had sailed by the Statue of Liberty and disembarked on Ellis Island. Most of them settled in the Lower East Side, a neighborhood that became known as the "Gateway to America." Many lived in crowded cold-water flats, observed the Sabbath, socialized on fire escapes, and eked out a living hunched over sewing machines fourteen hours a day in the sweatshops of the expanding fashion trade. At one time nothing but Yiddish was spoken for blocks in all directions.

Today, this is mostly just memories. The pushcarts have faded away, and many of the Jewish residents have dispersed throughout the city. Still, a subway ride to the neighborhood around Orchard Street, "the bargain district," is like a voyage back to Eastern Europe. It was Irving Berlin who commented: "Everybody ought to have a Lower East Side in their life."

Every Sunday the Orthodox Jews open their stores on Orchard Street for the first day of their business week. This is when bargain hunters hasten to rummage through the clothes racks and storefront bins. You can join in the fun by jostling your way through the pedestrians to the plethora of garments swinging overhead. Who knows? With a little chutzpah you might find just what you're looking for among the loads of luggage, leathergoods, and bolts of cloth piled on every available inch of space.

Have a yen for kosher victuals? You find places aplenty on the Lower East Side to please the palate. Katz's Delicatessen, at 205 East Houston, opened in 1888 and continues to carve corned beef and juicy pink pastrami by hand. During World War II, Katz's coined the slogan "Send a salami to your boy in the army!" Yonah Shimmel's Knishery, founded in 1910 at 175 East Houston, still supplies the neighborhood with flaky potato knishes, blintzes, borscht, and egg creams. Yum yum!

Now that your shopping bags are filled to overflowing, make a sojourn to the Lower East Side Tenement Museum at 97 Orchard Street. Constructed in 1863–1864 by Lucas Glockner, a German-born tailor, the building is now on the National Registry of Historic Places. A guided tour through the dark and dingy twenty-two-unit tenement—where artifacts were found beneath floorboards and behind layers of wallpaper—brings alive the harsh existence of the one thousand three hundred people who called it home during the years spanning 1863 to 1935. Just outside the museum, Guss' Pickles sells the sour green giants from orange barrels lining the sidewalk. You get what you bargain for on Orchard Street. You get to see, smell, hear, touch, and taste all of the magical ingredients that produced "Monkey Business," "Rhapsody in Blue," and "God Bless America."

Mulberry Street

AFICIONADOS OF NEOPOLITAN CUISINE should make a beeline for Mulberry Street. Here in this boisterous byway of Little Italy you can enjoy all of the delectable dishes you would expect to find in the sun-splashed villages along the Bay of Naples. One glance at the montage of salumerias and trattorias, of smiling signoras poking plump elbows out of tenement windows along with the alfresco aroma of peppers and sausages frying, and you come to realize that Italian culture has a firm foothold on Manhattan Island.

The perfect place to say "arrivederci" to a trim waistline is Paolucci's Restaurant at 149 Mulberry, around the corner from the imperial dome of the former police headquarters building. This prestigious old spaghetti palace is located in the parlor of the Stephen Van Rensselaer house. Built in 1816 as the town house for the upstate patroon family well before the massive migration from the boot-shaped peninsula began in 1885, it is a fine example of a modest Federal house complete with gambrel roof and dormers. Inside the landmark—opened by Donato Paolucci in 1947—you might order zuppa di mussel followed by pork chops Pileggi accompanied by a bottle of Pinot Grigio.

Parked across the street is Vinny's Nut House on wheels. It's a sure bet that the proprietor will coax you into trying a jaw-breaking chunk of imported torrone, a nougat confection of almonds and egg whites in a sugar paste.

One block west at 119 Mott, you arrive at the Original Vincent's Restaurant, situated there since 1904, when Guiseppe and Carmela Siano first established the eatery and named it after their son. That same year Carmela introduced her secret old-world recipe for the internationally celebrated Vincent's sauce. Today, gregarious Vincent Generoso concocts three kinds—sweet, medium, and hot—all served in his squeaky-clean dining room crowded with photographs of celebrities, politicians, and sports figures.

Some of the other gastronomic gems along Manhattan's Appian Way are Puglia's, noted far and wide for its pasta fazool, to be eaten family-style at long tables; and Luna's, where you can admire a painting of Mount Vesuvius. The painting may not win any prizes, but the lobster fra diavolo very well might! At the sparkling cafés along Mulberry, such as Ferrara's at 108–110, you can enjoy a fragrant, full-bodied espresso or cappuccino with a heaping serving of cannoli. *Buon appetito!*

If you have a passion for both the outdoors and eating, there is an eleven-day feast of viands on Mulberry during the annual Feast of San Gennaro. At this mid-September event honoring Saint Januarius, the patron saint of Napoli, you might play a game and win a kewpie doll, or sample such fare as meatball heroes, eggplant parmigiana, and zeppole, which are doughnuts sprinkled with powdered sugar. These delights await you in the brightly lit booths that line the green-white-and-red-flag-festooned street.

When you have had your fill of this festive forum, you can play bocce, the Italian version of lawn bowling, in one of the nearby squares. Or you might simply stroll up to Prince Street, where the old Saint Patrick's Cathedral proudly stands. Built in 1809, it was New York's first Roman Catholic cathedral. But for food lovers, nothing can outshine the cheerful Italian restaurants, cafés, shops, and many dialects on magical Mulberry Street.

SoHo

CARE TO MEET THE crusty old great-grandfathers of the glass-walled skyscrapers that tower over Manhattan Island today? If you do, then wander through the cast-iron district better known as SoHo because of its location south of Houston—pronounced "How-ston"—Street. Here, within a twenty-six-block area bounded by Houston, Canal, Crosby, and West Broadway, lies the largest concentration of post–Civil War cast-iron-fronted structures in New York, if not the world.

What exactly is cast-iron architecture? This product of the Industrial Revolution, developed and patented in 1848 by engraver and watchmaker James Bogardus, refers as much to the method of modular construction as to an architectural style. It involves iron buildings whose highly ornamental facades of Doric, Ionic, and Corinthian columns were cast in New York foundries, transported to the building site, then bolted together to form the final structure. When completed, these early prefabs looked so much like stone structures that most passersby had no idea they were made of iron.

The creation of SoHo's unique concentration of architecture was almost entirely due to the building boom that followed the Civil War. By then Broadway had become a street of fashionable stores, with the so-called Ladies' Mile stretching from Wanamaker's on Tenth Street, past Tiffany's and Lord & Taylor, and as far north as Twenty-third Street. The district flourished as the center of the notions and dry-goods trade until the 1890s. Then cast-iron fronts went into decline due to a series of disastrous fires.

Fashions change, and when the big merchants moved uptown, small industries replaced them in the roomy lofts. In the years that followed, SoHo's bumpy Belgian block pavements became so crowded with pushcarts and dealers that it was almost impossible to penetrate, and the fire department labeled it "Hell's Hundred Acres." It wasn't until the 1960s that artists seeking low rents and lofty ceilings to accommodate their large canvases and bulky sculptures discovered SoHo. In 1970, the city legalized residential use of lofts in commercial buildings by artists, and since then the area has enjoyed a cultural renaissance.

By far the best way to explore the district is to walk south on Broadway. At the corner of Broome Street your eyes sweep across one of the brightest gems in SoHo's cast-iron crown. This is the E. V. Haughwout & Company building, painted in Turkish drab, designed by John P. Gaynor and fabricated by Daniel Badger's Architectural Iron Works. Built in 1857 for a merchant of cut glass, china, silverware, and chandeliers, this flamboyant five-story structure with its Palladian rhythms has been called the Parthenon of cast-iron buildings. The first practical safety elevator in a commercial building was installed here by Elisha Graves Otis in 1857, paving the way for taller offspring to come.

Though the most distinguished buildings are on Broadway, such as the Singer building at 561, the blocks to the west offer the visitor a quintessential cast-iron landscape. The best streets in which to enjoy this are Greene, Broome, Grand, Mercer, Prince, and Spring. Here you can admire the arches and brackets, the fancy capitals and fluted columns affixed to these pseudo-Venetian palaces festooned with fire escapes, that few pedestrians even bother to look at. Manhattan Island's metal-and-glass skyscrapers are direct descendants of these Italianate-style structures.

Charlton-King-Vandam

ONE OF THE MOST surprising sights for the city wanderer can be found near factory-filled Varick Street and hyperactive Avenue of the Americas, on Charlton, King, and Vandam Streets. This minute-size, well-preserved pocket of old New York, built on the site of Aaron Burr's country seat, Richmond Hill, contains the greatest collection of Federal-style row houses in the city. To walk these three unspoiled and unchanged streets is to experience a delightful and dramatic step into the past.

Richmond Hill, built in 1767 for Major Abraham Mortier, was one of the most magnificent mansions ever to grace Manhattan Island. Situated on a hilltop, this Georgian house with its pillared porch enjoyed an impressive view of the Hudson River. During the Revolutionary War, General Washington used it as his headquarters. When New York was the capital of the thirteen original states, it served as the vice-presidential mansion for John Adams. Later, Aaron Burr bought it and lavishly entertained in it to further his political ambitions. Here, he skilled himself in the use of the pistol "by dint of daily practice for the purpose of meeting Alexander Hamilton in a duel," the result of which was the death of Hamilton. This event caused such ill feeling against Burr that he was obliged to flee the city. His estate was then taken over by John Jacob Astor, the great fur trader and real estate magnate. With the development of the city northward, Astor decided to create an instant town by building houses on lots measuring 25 by 100 feet. In 1820 the mansion was moved, the hill leveled, the lots laid out, and the houses started.

The neighborhood was originally tenanted by prosperous builders, lawyers, and merchants. In the years that followed, while nearby streets sank into slums or became commercial, the Charlton-King-Vandam district remained settled and serene. A number of houses were kept in the same family for generations, and many people who led lives of distinction in the city continued to live there. Because all of the residences were built by one owner within a few years of one another and show such exceptional harmony, the district, according to the Landmarks Preservation Commission, "represents an extraordinary architectural and historic document."

Today, you find what is probably the longest row of Federal and early Greek Revival houses in Manhattan on the north side of Charlton. Nowhere else does there exist such a continuity of style as the rosy-brick residences at Nos. 37 and 39. With their detailed doorways and leaded-glass sidelights, the Greek Revival dwellings at Nos. 20, 40, 42, and 44 King Street, circa 1840, are almost perfectly preserved, creating an impressive streetscape. Astor himself, the richest man in America at the time, owned the house with the garnet-red door at No. 43 King Street in 1828, sold it that same year, and repurchased it in 1840, just eight years before his death. Vandam Street offers on its north side an unbroken row of fine Federal dwellings, circa 1823. Almost all of them, like those at Nos. 23, 25, 27, and 29, still retain their pitched roofs, multiwindowed dormers, tall chimneys, and intricate ironwork.

You can walk all you want around this enclave of early-nineteenth-century New York. But keep in mind that although it is considered to be part of Greenwich Village, it is officially Charlton-King-Vandam, and its loyal residents won't let you forget that fact for a minute.

St. Luke's Place

BROWSING ABOUT THIS BLOCK of nineteenth-century brick and brownstone Italianate residences woven together by cast-iron balustrades, smothered by wisteria vines, and shaded by shiny green gingko trees, you might expect to see a horse and carriage come clip-clopping along. Or you might not be at all surprised to see a Stutz Bearcat roadster cruising around the corner to deposit dapper Jimmy Walker, mayor of New York during the Roaring Twenties, at his four-story town house, No. 6 St. Luke's Place. Lit by the "mayor's lamps," a tradition that dates from the early Dutch days when lanterns were placed outside the homes of city officials, this short lane can evoke more memories of happy-go-lucky days-gone-by than almost any other on Manhattan Island.

Possibly because it is one of the most splendid streets in the city, St. Luke's Place also happens to be one of the most difficult to find. Situated at the southwestern corner of Greenwich Village, it is tucked between Hudson Street and Seventh Avenue South, north of Clarkson and south of Morton. Its physical isolation has enabled the neighborhood to maintain a distinctive character, an elaborate stage set where Ziegfeld Follies girls once guzzled champagne behind parlor-floor French windows and fountains, deep in English ivy, gurgled in back-yard gardens.

It was here at No. 12 St. Luke's Place, across the street from James Walker Park, that Sherwood Anderson, the playwright, livened things up in 1922. Two doors down at No. 16 Theodore Dreiser worked on *An American Tragedy*. And in between, at No. 14, Marianne Moore, the Pulitzer Prize–winning poet and faithful fan of

"Dem Bums," the old Brooklyn Dodgers, resided from 1918 to 1929.

But it was jovial Jimmy Walker—"Beau James" as he was called by his friends and flocks of admirers—who set St. Luke's Place aglow with excitement. Here the bow-tied playboy, whose antics and wisecracks diverted the nation and whose closets held more than two hundred suits and thirty-seven pairs of shoes, held court during the zany days of F. Scott Fitzgerald, who penned *The Great Gatsby*, and his wife, Zelda.

It was an intoxicating time when Prohibition was foiled by fun-loving, diamond-wearing flappers and gentlemen who preferred blondes. Those were the halcyon days when Babe Ruth, "the Sultan of Swat," was smacking home runs out of Yankee Stadium; when Charles Lindbergh, "the Lone Eagle," was being treated to a ticker-tape parade up Broadway, celebrating his 1927 solo flight from New York to Paris; when cigar-chomping Al Smith, "the Happy Warrior," was campaigning for the presidency in a brown derby.

On October 24, 1929, the stock market crashed, and the days of quickly won wealth on Wall Street and the social whirl of making whoopee in speakeasies fizzled as fast as you can say "Jimmy Walker." The debonair man-about-town who spent more time at racetracks, in nightclubs, and on pleasure cruises than he did at city hall was finally forced to resign, taking his cane and boutonniere on a permanent vacation. Now the twenties' roar has subsided to a mere whisper. But the residences built in the 1850s on St. Luke's Place still stand, framed by gingko trees that sway in the soft summer breeze, telling tales of a wonderful town when it was young and foolish. ✍

Grove Court

DUSTING OFF THE BOOKSHELF, you may come across a dog-eared copy of O. Henry's short stories. In it you're bound to find "The Last Leaf," a charming story about a lovely young woman who is lying in her sickbed waiting out the days until the last leaf on the vine outside her window falls to the ground. A dashing artist, who has been courting her, wards off the tragedy by painting a leaf on the wall as she sleeps. When the leaf and the stem stubbornly refuse to leave the vine, the heroine regains her health, the hero proposes marriage, and the couple lives happily ever after.

The story goes that O. Henry, who lived in the neighborhood, got the idea for this romantic tale from a visit he made to Grove Court, six small three-story houses slumbering behind an antique iron gate in a remote section of Greenwich Village. These barn-red dwellings, set off by chalk-white shutters, were built over the stone basements of what were two seventeenth-century Dutch farmhouses. These were once situated quite close to the Hudson River, which was named for the navigator who sailed up it aboard the Dutch ship *Half Moon* in 1609. These Dutch dwellings burned to the ground, probably during the fires that destroyed the city during the revolution. The present houses were built over their charred foundations around 1853.

Looking through the gate today from a bend between Nos. 10 and 12 Grove Street, you discover a tree-shaded, ivy-covered courtyard paved with moss-covered bricks that ripple like waves. At one time this private pedestrian-only plot of land was called Pig's Alley. At another more boisterous time it was known as Mixed Ale Alley. Now everyone calls it Grove Court, and you won't find a more peaceful enclave in all New York. Some citizens say that this parcel of early Dutch real estate remains the quietest residential area in Manhattan and one with a whisper of graciousness.

The houses, which look as though they were taken down brick by brick and brought over by barge from Bruges, Belgium, are now all owner-occupied. At one point in time sculptors Alan and Robert Robbins, who had lived in the court since their childhood, remembered when the old Ninth Avenue El, with its Swiss chaletlike stationhouses and windows glowing with blue and red Bohemian glass, was within walking distance. Other residents have included a descendant of one of the founders of the New York Stock Exchange and a congenial group of photographers, writers, and artists.

Just a heartbeat away from the court stands the church of St. Luke-in-the-Fields at 485 Hudson Street between Barrow and Christopher. In 1822, when this blush-pink brick church was built, it was called St. Luke's Episcopal Chapel of Trinity Parish. It was restored after a fire in 1981. On the south side of the chapel, noted for its soaring Palladian windows of bottled glass beneath a square tower, dozes an old-fashioned garden. When you visit there on a lazy summer afternoon with the roses at their rambling best, you have to pinch yourself to realize that you are standing in the center of one of America's largest cities. The vicarage to the north of the chapel is the oldest existing in New York.

In 1952, the antique bricks and native stones of Grove Court were almost swept away to make room for an asphalt-topped playground. But, thanks to the people who fought to preserve it, this last vestige of old New York will go on gathering moss for many years to come.

Bedford Street

REMEMBER EDNA ST. VINCENT MILLAY, the golden-haired, green-eyed poet who boasted, "My candle burns at both ends"? Certainly one of the most romantic figures in Greenwich Village in the 1920s, she lived in 1923–24 at No. 75½ Bedford Street, otherwise known as the "Narrowest House in the Village." A pilgrimage to this higgledy-piggledy house with Dutch-stepped gables between Morton and Commerce will afford you a look at storybook New York.

The brick-faced diminutive dwelling where the petite poet-in-residence wrote the Pulitzer Prize–winning *The Ballad of the Harp Weaver* is only 9½ feet wide and 39 feet deep. It was originally constructed in 1873 to span an alley to the rear court, where the main entrance was. Though narrow by most standards, it was wide enough to allow a horse and buggy to pass through. The three-story house was the ideal setting for the irreverent poet who made her national reputation with the publication of the poem "Renascence" when she was only nineteen years old. She arrived in the Village in 1917 to illuminate Bohemian society with her savage beauty and intoxicating voice.

Next door at No. 77 Bedford is the old Isaacs-Hendricks house, which was built in 1799 for Joshua Isaacs on property purchased from Elbert Roosevelt. In 1801, Isaacs's son-in-law, Harmond Hendricks, a copper merchant, bought the clapboard-sided structure, and it was held by the Hendricks family until 1928.

Winding your way off Bedford and on to Commerce Street, you arrive at a one-of-a-kind pair of rosy-brick houses with mansard roofs at Nos. 39 and 41, which proclaim the elegance that once surrounded this ancient quarter. Legend has it that the twin residences, separated by a small garden thick with shrubs, were built around 1831 by a sea captain for his two spoiled daughters, one for each because they did not get along very well with each other.

Arriving back on Bedford at the corner of Grove, a trio of houses that look like a stage setting for Hansel and Gretel come into view. The clapboard building with russet shutters was once the home of William Hyde, a sashmaker. Built in 1822, it is probably the best-preserved wood-frame house in Greenwich Village today. Hiding behind it is Hyde's workshop at No. 100 Bedford. The tall timber-and-tan-stucco building with the high-pitched roofs looming over it at No. 102, called "Twin Peaks," was put up around 1830 and renovated in 1925.

Farther up at No. 86 Bedford, if you can possibly find it, Chumley's awaits. During its Prohibition days, it was disguised as a garage and served as a speakeasy handing out the hard stuff in coffee cups. Over the years Chumley's attracted such prolific writers as Dashiell Hammett, who wrote *The Maltese Falcon*, and John Steinbeck, who penned the classic *The Grapes of Wrath*. You needn't whisper "Joe sent me" to gain admission to the dusky dining room lined with dust jackets of bestselling books. But try not to step on one of the chubby pups stretched out on the barroom floor.

The bright flame that was Edna St. Vincent Millay flickered out on October 18, 1950, but her poems are still praised for their spirit and genius. It is no wonder then that her diminutive Dutch dollhouse and all the other ones surrounding it on Bedford Street still give such a lovely light. 🖋

Patchin Place

THE BEST WAY TO FERRET OUT this cul-de-sac in the crazy-quilt pattern of Greenwich Village streets is to look for the clock tower of the Jefferson Market Courthouse, which monopolizes the corner of West Tenth Street and the Avenue of the Americas. This turreted castle, straight out of *Cinderella*, was built in 1876 to serve as the women's court, but it now houses a public library behind its multicolored stained-glass windows. On a sunny day it casts a Victorian-Gothic shadow onto Patchin Place, which dozes directly opposite.

When you stop at the bishop's-crook light pole and peer through the gate, you get a glimpse of how New York looked back in the nineteenth century. Both Patchin Place and the adjoining Milligan Place, a triangular court containing four houses fronting on the west side of the Avenue of the Americas, are named for the original owners of the property, once part of Sir Peter Warren's farm. The tract was sold to Samuel Milligan in 1799. He conveyed it in 1848, at about the time the little row houses were built, to one Aaron D. Patchin, husband of Milligan's daughter, Isabelle. Patchin's granddaughter, Grace Ingersoll Patchin Stuart, owned the property until 1920.

There was a time when these 150-year-old flats, their oyster-gray facades broken by a filigree of fire escapes, served as second-class boardinghouses for the Basque waiters who worked at the beautiful Brevoort House Hotel on Fifth Avenue, long since gone. Later the buildings were divided into forty-five apartments, all with cheerful fireplaces. It was then that Patchin Place began to play an important role in the Village's legendary Bohemian days of the 1920s and 1930s.

The little blind alley with its ten houses became the hideaway of a number of well-known writers. e. e. cummings, the poet, wrote and painted for over forty years in his top-floor studio at No. 4. John Reed, the Communist and journalist, penned *10 Days That Shook the World* after having an affair with Mabel Dodge, the chatelaine of a salon of "movers and shakers," in her apartment at One Fifth Avenue. Other renowned residents of this village-within-a-village have been John Masefield, England's poet laureate; Harry Kemp, the "Hobo Poet"; and Eugene O'Neill, the playwright who wrote *Long Day's Journey into Night*. One block east at No. 15 West Tenth Street once stood the Studio Building. Modeled on French ateliers and designed by Richard Morris Hunt, it was built specifically for artists. Here, John LaFarge, Albert Bierstadt, and Winslow Homer worked at their easels.

Over the years, determined and ingenious tenants of Patchin and Milligan have forestalled all attempts by land developers and real estate tycoons to turn their homes into what cummings called "hugely hideous hyperboxes teeming with moneyed subhumanity." Happily, both places have survived the wrecker's ball and the bulldozer, and they retain to this day their unique personality.

After a neighborhood shopping excursion to Balducci's to pinch the plums, then to Jefferson Market to select one of their savory salads, you might find the solitude of the ancient alley somewhat shattering. Shaded by ailanthus trees, the Chinese "trees of heaven," Patchin Place has provided the right kind of creative climate to nourish the pens of rebels and heroes, the great and the near-great. Its relaxed rhythm and quiet charm make it one of New York's most cherished byways. ✍

MacDougal Alley

WITH *COMMON SENSE* THOMAS PAINE as their trailblazer, a revolutionary array of artists and writers has been attracted to the archaic alleyways of Greenwich Village. Herman Melville, who caught the public eye with *Moby-Dick* in 1851, worked in the Gansevoort meat market on Fourteenth Street. James Fenimore Cooper, author of *The Last of the Mohicans,* lived on Bleecker Street in the area once called Sappokanican by the Native Americans. Edgar Allan Poe penned his tales on Carmine Street. Willa Cather scribbled *Shadows on the Rock* in the Grosvenor Hotel. Mark Twain enjoyed the good life on Tenth Street, as did poet Emma Lazarus, who wrote "give me your huddled masses" for the inscription on the Statue of Liberty. Dylan Thomas, the curly-haired Welsh poet who created *Under Milkwood* and whooped it up in the White Horse Tavern, died at Saint Vincent's Hospital on November 9, 1953, just days after his thirty-ninth birthday. To walk these streets today is an adventure in nostalgia.

An enchanting spot to start your excursion is MacDougal Alley, hiding in the heart of Greenwich Village, between West Eighth Street and Washington Square. Named for Alexander MacDougal, a noted Son of Liberty, it is one of the few cul-de-sacs that have survived from the last century. Originally, the alley was lined with the carriage houses and stables that belonged to the elegant mansions facing the verdant square. Then in the early part of the twentieth century, it became the stomping ground for artists and writers who converted the buildings into sky-lighted studios and snug living quarters.

In the northwest corner house lived sculptor James Earle Fraser, who designed the old buffalo nickel. Jackson Pollock, who splattered paint on canvases and created works hung in the Museum of Modern Art, had a workshop here. Sculptor Jo Davidson was a resident as well. Today, stopping by at daylight or dusk, you come upon a scene from Dylan Thomas's native Wales: timber-and-brick cottages with bay windows, bombazine-black chimney pots, and purple clematis vines growing profusely around front doorways.

Around the corner, the stately town houses backing up to the alley and comprising Washington Square North create a stark contrast. When constructed in 1831, a few years after the old potter's field opposite was converted into a park and parade ground, these gracious relics of a fading past were owned by New Yorkers prominent in literary circles. Henry James, who immortalized the Village block with his celebrated novel *Washington Square,* frequently visited his grandmother's home in the row. Edith Wharton wrote her novels at No. 7.

Walking west on Washington Place and past No. 82, where African-American novelist Richard Wright wrote *Native Son,* you arrive at the Avenue of the Americas. Just across the street stands Saint Joseph's, a church in the Greek Revival style with a dominant Doric colonnade. Built in 1833, it is the oldest Roman Catholic sanctuary in the city. Here, behind the main altar and illuminated by Waterford crystal chandeliers from Ireland, is a fresco, *The Transfiguration of Jesus,* which some say may be the oldest mural in America.

Despite all the changes that have occurred elsewhere in the city, MacDougal Alley and the nostalgic streets that stem from it still have, as Henry James so aptly put it, "a kind of established repose, the look of having had something of history."

Washington Mews

Every spring the sidewalks, stoops, fence posts, and fire escapes surrounding Washington Square blossom with eye-catching canvases, wild watercolors, still lifes, and sculptures. What's happening? It's the Washington Square Outdoor Art Exhibit, a perennial favorite with Greenwich Village pedestrians. This colorful exhibit attracts multitudes of art lovers in search of a masterpiece hiding in a doorway or hanging on a garden gate. If you should be one of the crowd ambling among the artists and easels, you might stumble upon a Belgian-block-paved alleyway snuggled between University Place and Fifth Avenue and south of East Eighth Street. Here, you'll find thirty small stucco carriage houses that could be pictured on a postcard mailed from Majorca or Málaga. This can only be Washington Mews, a hop, skip, and puddle jump from Stanford White's Washington Arch, where Fifth Avenue comes to an elaborate end.

Awaiting the artist is an ideal motif for brush, pen, charcoal, or colored pencil: two rows of tiny dwellings, inset with colored tiles, slumbering under blankets of ivy and wisteria vines. The five houses on the north side of the mews, once called Shinbone Alley, were originally built as stables in 1833 for the residents of Washington Square North, whose yards extended to the far side of what is now a private street. The remodeling of the stables into homes and studios was done in 1916 for Sailors Snug Harbor, owners of the land. It was then that the other houses with whitewashed facades were added. The dwellings on the south side with a similar architectural motif were constructed in 1939. With doors painted in welcoming shades of bottle green, burgundy red, and azure blue and brightened by brass door knockers, these houses had such distinguished occupants as political pundit Walter Lippmann and Grover Whalen, the city's official greeter during the 1939 World's Fair. The converted stable with the shell-pink door at No. 60 was once the studio of Gertrude Vanderbilt Whitney, the renowned sculptor who founded the art museum that bears her name.

How the exhibit got started is a story in itself. One spring day during the Depression, a penniless artist picked up his palette and began to paint a picture in one of the streets off the square. As his canvas took shape, a passerby stopped, admired the work, and offered to buy it on the spot. Afterward, the painter, his pockets lined with silver, gathered a group of artist friends together, and they decided to exhibit their work in Washington Square. Later, with the assistance of Gertrude Whitney, the Washington Square Outdoor Art Exhibit opened in 1931, the first of its kind in the country. It is now held twice a year, in late May and early September.

Ever since Evert Duyckinck arrived from Holland in 1638 and began painting the Dutch burgomasters wearing high white collars, Manhattan has been a magnet for artists. Gilbert Charles Stuart painted his first portrait of George Washington here before moving his studio to Germantown, Pennsylvania, in 1796, where he went on to do portraits of Presidents Jefferson, Madison, and John Adams. William Glackens of the Ashcan school and Edward Hopper captured the everyday lives of New Yorkers with bold brushstrokes in the early 1900s. This tradition is sure to continue as long as there are motifs like Washington Mews to capture the artist's eye and imagination.

Hudson

W N

S E

West Side Highway

Tenth Avenue

Chelsea Square

W 23 W 34 W 42

Amsterdam

Broadway

Strawberry Fields

Grove Court

Bedford St

St. Luke's Place

Patchin Place

Seventh Avenue

86 W

W 72

Charlton~King~Van Dam

Sixth Avenue

CENTRAL

Washington Mews

Fifth Avenue

FIFTH

Washington Harrison St. Houses

Macdougal Alley

W Broadway

Soho

Broadway

E 23

E 12

E 59

E 72

Colonnade Row

Gramercy Park

Mott St

Cooper Square

E 34

South St Seaport

Mulberry St

Third Ave

Sniffen Court

THIRD

Stuyvesant St.

First Ave

Treadwell Farm

Franklin D. Roosevelt Drive

Beekman Place

FIRST

Orchard St.

East River

MANHATTAN ISLAND

Brooklyn

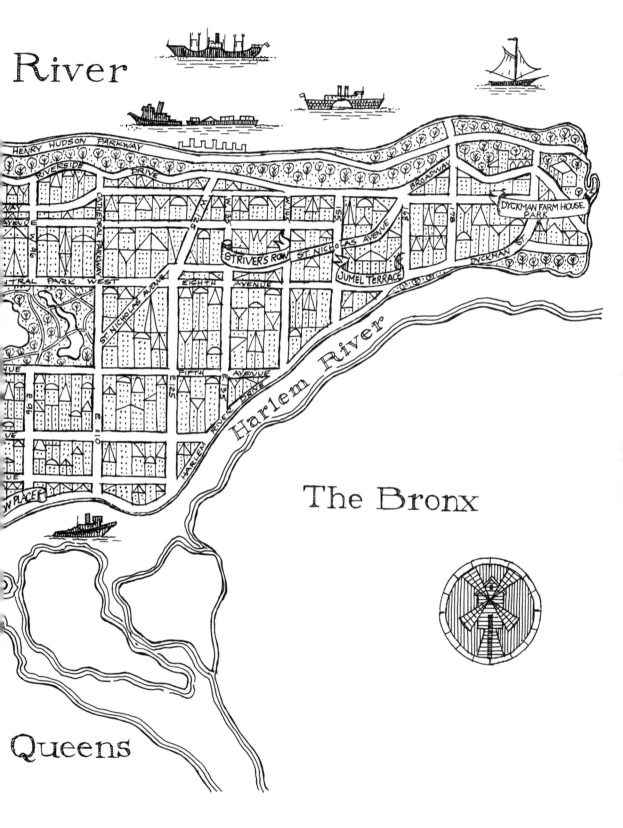

River

Queens

The Bronx

Harlem River

HENRY HUDSON PARKWAY
RIVERSIDE DRIVE
CATHEDRAL PARKWAY
CENTRAL PARK WEST
ST. NICHOLAS AVENUE
EIGHTH AVENUE
FIFTH AVENUE
HARLEM RIVER DRIVE
BROADWAY
DYCKMAN ST.
STRIVER'S ROW
ST. NICHOLAS AVENUE
JUMEL TERRACE
DYCKMAN FARM HOUSE PARK
W. 146
W. 151
W. 139
W. 155
E. 125
E. 96
PLACE

Colonnade Row

LOOKING AS THOUGH it was spirited from the Rue de la Concorde in Paris, the elegant two-story Corinthian colonnade evokes the classical grandeur of Greece's golden era. It was the first and only complex of its kind in New York that unified a number of town houses behind one great facade. It is La Grange Terrace—better known as Colonnade Row—at 428-434 Lafayette Street, one of the timeworn treasures of New York's architectural heritage and a noble example of neighborhood planning.

La Grange Terrace was built in 1832 by Seth Geer, who named it after the Château de La Grange, which is located outside Paris and belonged to the French patriot the Marquis de Lafayette. When completed in 1833, the colonnade comprised nine town houses with twenty-six pillars. Geer's speculative venture in constructing magnificent houses such a distance from town was regarded as rather foolish at that time. But his investment was soon justified, as Lafayette Place, which cut through the old Vauxhall Gardens to Astor Place, became a residential district for prominent New Yorkers of the day.

The construction of the colonnade was not without problems. It seems that the convicts at Sing Sing not only quarried the Westchester marble for the buildings, they cut and prepared it as well. This economy aroused the stonecutters of the city. They paraded through the streets carrying banners that insisted "Down with convict labor." Finally, they caused a riot, making it necessary for the city to call out the militia. Residences were soon built on every side, including the Old Merchant's House, that Greek Revival classic at No. 29 East Fourth Street where Seabury Tredwell lived in 1832. The dwelling stands today exactly as

it did then both inside and out. Notable residents of the colonnade were John Jacob Astor and David Gardiner, whose daughter, Julia, married John Tyler soon after he became America's tenth president in 1841. But the row's most celebrated tenant was Washington Irving, who wrote the bawdiest and best-loved books ever written about New York.

The story goes that the pomposity of New York's first guidebook, written by Dr. Samuel L. Mitchill in 1807, greatly amused Irving. He was also astonished to learn how few citizens realized that the city had once been called New Amsterdam. So, with tongue in cheek, Irving wrote *A History of New York from the Beginning of the World to the End of the Dutch Dynasty*. It poked fun at the Dutch and was an instant success with readers of English ancestry. Because he pretended it had been written by an antiquarian named Diedrich Knickerbocker, his parody became known as *Knickerbocker's History of New York*. It also gave the city its beloved symbol: Father Knickerbocker.

Directly across Lafayette at No. 425 one finds the Joseph Papp Public Theatre, site of the New York Shakespeare Festival. This imposing Italianate structure, completed in 1881, was built by John Jacob Astor as the Astor Library, the city's first major library broadly accessible to the public.

Alas, if Washington Irving were alive today, he would be saddened to discover that only four of the original town houses in La Grange Terrace survive in the twenty-first century. The other five met their Waterloo years ago. Yet despite the grime collected over the years, Colonnade Row, with its French doors, wreath-adorned fenestrations, and thirteen fluted Corinthian columns, still overpowers you with its classical extravagance and originality. ✍♥

Cooper Square

WITH THE IRISH POTATO FAMINE of 1846–47 dark upon the land, more than one million starving people immigrated from Ireland to the United States. Coming from Celtic thatched-roofed cottages on windswept farms in Galway and Glendalough, Cork and Kilkenny, they filled the ship's steerage, arrived in Castle Garden, and settled near the area now called Cooper Square. Taking jobs as laborers, they swung the picks, lifted the shovels, and brought down the hammers that transformed New York from a city the size of Dublin to America's mightiest metropolis.

The home, the church, and the saloon were the centers of life around the square in the East Village at East Eighth Street and Fourth Avenue. This is where Peter Cooper—inventor of the "Tom Thumb," America's first functioning steam engine—established the Cooper Union for the Advancement of Science and Art in 1859. The philanthropist believed that education should be "as free as water or air" to immigrants and the children of the working class. It was in the Great Hall of Cooper Union on February 27, 1860, that Abraham Lincoln delivered his "right makes might" speech, in which he set forth his antislavery platform. Just south of the city's first steel-frame building lies a triangular park where you can sit on a bench and admire the bronze statue of the industrialist, created by the Irish-born sculptor Augustus Saint-Gaudens.

Care for a bite of corned beef and cabbage and a mug or two of amber ale? Then head across Fourth Avenue to 15 East Seventh Street, where McSorley's Old Ale House has been going strong since 1854. Founded by John McSorley, a native of County Tyrone, he furnished the place with a long ebony and mahogany bar, gas lamps, and a potbellied stove. He brewed his own cream stock ale and porter. The tavern became a bit of heaven away from the "old sod." Today, it's no blarney when they tell you that McSorley's is one of the oldest and most-beloved saloons in the city.

A visit to this Gaelic landmark is worth the price of a platter of sharp cheese, sliced Bermuda onions, and a stack of salty crackers. To sit at one of the battered tables in the back room, opposite a provocative painting of a golden nude gazing at a green parrot, is to go back to a time when friendly sons of Saint Patrick with thick brogues sang "I'll Take You Home Again, Kathleen."

Old John McSorley considered it impossible for men to drink with any tranquillity in the presence of the "daughters of Eve." So for years a notice was kept nailed to the front door reading NO BACK ROOM IN HERE FOR LADIES. Alas, women's lib won out in 1971, and fair ladies were finally admitted to the all-male preserve.

Mutton-chopped McSorley had a mania for memorabilia. For years he saved the wishbones of holiday turkeys and hung them on a rod connecting a pair of gas lamps over the bar. He covered every inch of space with sepia prints of presidents, politicians, and picnic outings. The dust-covered chair that once belonged to Peter Cooper, the benevolent patron, can still be seen behind the cluttered bar along with fading photographs of President John F. Kennedy. So the next time you go carousing around Cooper Square, stop in at McSorley's to find that "Ale is Well" and Irish eyes are still smilin'.

Stuyvesant Street

THE MOST PICTURESQUE CHARACTER ever to set foot on Manhattan Island was probably hard-swearing Peter Stuyvesant, sometimes called "Old Silvernails," because the stick of wood that stood in place of his right leg was decorated with silver nails. He governed New Amsterdam from 1647 to 1664. During his tenure as the last Dutch governor general, Stuyvesant owned a country residence two miles north of his Whitehall town house, known as the Bouwerie, or farm. It covered many acres from what is now Fourth Avenue to the banks of the East River. When Stuyvesant died in 1672, his remains were interred in the family vault beneath the little chapel dedicated to Saint Nicholas, which he had built on the farm in 1660.

The Bouwerie, with its windmills, weathercocks, orchards, and haystacks, vanished from the Manhattan landscape centuries ago. But standing in its place today at the end of Stuyvesant Street is Saint Mark's-in-the-Bouwerie, the oldest site of continuous worship in New York. A visit to the historic churchyard is the best way to acquaint yourself with the early generations of the Stuyvesant family, which represents, more than any other family, Dutch New York.

Walking east on Stuyvesant Street, you can't help but admire one of the finest early Federal-style residences in the city. This is the Stuyvesant-Fish House at No. 21, an early nineteenth-century dwelling that is noted for its unusually ample width. Petrus Stuyvesant, a great-grandson of the Dutch governor general, built this dwelling in 1804 for his daughter Elizabeth, who married Revolutionary war hero Major Nicholas Fish. Their son, Hamilton, was born in 1808 and went on to enjoy a successful career as governor of New York, U.S. senator, and President Ulysses S. Grant's secretary of state. Next door begins a charming group of brick and brownstone row houses called "The Triangle." Not only do they form one, but their appearance is similar to the bow of a massive clipper ship sailing into the east wind. These elegant residences of the 1850s are attributed to the architect James Renwick, Jr.

At the juncture of East Tenth Street and Second Avenue, you arrive at the entrance to the churchyard of Saint Mark's, which is flanked by statues of two Native Americans. The Bradford pear-tree-shaded yard is paved with marble tablets marking the vaults of such old New York families as the Schermerhorns, the Vanden Heuvels, the Ingersolls, and the Wotherspoons. Just inside the side gate you are greeted by a bust of Peter Stuyvesant, given to the city by Wilhelmina, Queen of the Netherlands. You are next attracted to a blackened stone tablet affixed to the eastern wall of the church, which reads: "In this vault, lies buried Petrus Stuyvesant, late Captain General and Governor in Chief of Amsterdam in New Netherlands, now called New York and the Dutch West India Islands. Died February A.D. 1672, aged 80 years."

Saint Mark's is an edifice that was constructed over a considerable period of time. The fieldstone nave with its arched windows was consecrated in 1799 and so belongs to the Georgian period. The steeple, which went up in 1828, is Greek Revival, and the cast-iron front porch, added in 1858, is in the Italianate tradition. Not surprisingly, all these diverse elements harmonize remarkably well, which should please the grouchy Dutchman with the silver-inlaid wooden leg as he rests peacefully beneath his beloved Bouwerie.

Chelsea Square

REMEMBER AS A CHILD being read *A Visit from St. Nicholas* on a snowy night before Christmas? Well, Clement Clarke Moore, the man credited for writing the fifty-six-line classic for his wife and eight children in December 1822, donated one choice block of his family's estate, Chelsea House, as the site for the General Theological Seminary. It functions today as the focal point for Chelsea Square.

When Moore was born on July 15, 1779, the area resembled a primitive landscape painting with rolling green hills, apple orchards, and country lanes edged with tall elms. In 1830, realizing that his beloved birthplace was going to be leveled due to the city commissioner's plan of 1811 for a grid street pattern, Moore immediately began to envision an elegant neighborhood that would take its place. He created a community where "purchasers . . . will be required to build fireproof houses of good quality. Those on the avenue lots to be three stories and those on the cross streets, two stories in height." Here, in the heart of his Chelsea community, Moore lived a rich and full life as a professor teaching Asian and Greek literature at the seminary.

After a period of steady decline in the early part of the twentieth century, Chelsea, with its wealth of fine old houses in the Greek Revival and Italianate styles, has been rediscovered as one of Manhattan's most enjoyable enclaves. A stroll through the Chelsea historical district acquaints you with Moore's cherished neighborhood.

The General Theological Seminary complex, covering a full city block and shaded by tall trees growing in quiet courtyards, plays an important role in the community's life. The English Collegiate Gothic architecture and the commanding bell tower, completed in 1888, lend a certain distinction to the Chelsea landscape. The playing of the carillon every afternoon and the call to vespers are traditions enjoyed by everyone within earshot.

Just north of the seminary at No. 401 West 21st Street sits a miniature building that can rightfully boast of being the second oldest in Chelsea. Erected in 1832, this is the only structure in the area retaining the proportions and characteristics of the Federal style. With its berry-red brick chimney, high-pitched roof, and snow-white shutters and sashes, it could rightly pose for anyone's Christmas card. As early as 1835, lively and quick Theodore Martine ran a grocery, flour, and feed store at this address.

What about the oldest house in Chelsea? Well, it can be found directly south of the seminary and is situated at No. 404 West 20th Street. This distinguished dwelling was constructed in 1830 for Hugh Walker on land leased from Moore for forty dollars a year. Next to it, Nos. 406 to 418 present a remarkable row of six-storied Greek Revival residences. They were constructed in 1840 for Don Alonzo Cushman, a parish leader who became a millionaire developing Chelsea. Known as "Cushman Row," with wreath-enclosed attic windows and handsome original detail, it is considered one of the finest examples of this style of architecture in New York.

At No. 414 West 22nd Street stands the James N. Wells mansion, circa 1835, the city's largest surviving Greek Revival dwelling. It is the only one with five bays and was remodeled in 1864–66 in the Italianate style fashionable at that time.

Gramercy Park

A HEARTY REPAST at Pete's Tavern is the best way to start an enjoyable jaunt through Gramercy Park. O. Henry wrote stories in the second booth of this vintage café, which is located on the corner of Irving Place and East 18th Street. Surrounded by balconied brownstones and fashionable clubs, where gentlemen once tipped top hats to ladies parading under parasols, this grande dame of New York parks is as close to the Gay Nineties as you can get in the twenty-first century.

With a formidable fence enclosing ancient trees and people on park benches feeding pampered pigeons, Gramercy Park can proudly claim that it is the city's sole privately owned square, open only to owners of the apartments and town houses that border it. The original deed provided that each of the lot holders have a key. The history of the park dates back to 1831, when Samuel B. Ruggles, a lawyer, purchased the marshy Crom Mess Hie area from the estate of James Duane, a Revolutionary patriot and first mayor of New York City after the war. Duane deeded sixty-six lots surrounding the enclosed green area, where the new owners were to build their handsome town houses.

Soon afterward, leading New Yorkers gravitated to Gramercy Park, including Stuyvesant Fish and architect Stanford White, who was killed by Pittsburgh millionaire Harry K. Thaw on the roof of Madison Square Garden. Samuel Tilden, governor of New York, lived at No. 15 on the south side of the park. Now the National Arts Club, it was designed by Calvert Vaux. The Players, at No. 16, is one of the most distinguished buildings on the square. The splendid portico was added by Stanford White soon after the blizzard of 1888. The house was bought from the widow of Clarkson N. Potter by the great actor, Edwin Booth, brother of Lincoln's assassin, John Wilkes Booth, who had it remodeled for the club. Just around the corner on Irving Place lived Elihu Root, secretary of state under President Theodore Roosevelt, who was born on October 27, 1858, in his family's brownstone town house at No. 28 East 20th Street. Teddy's home was torn down years later but was then completely rebuilt exactly like the original. It is now run by the National Park Service.

On the east side of the park at No. 34 towers The Gramercy, a terra-cotta fortresslike apartment house with turreted corners. Incorporated in 1883, it is the oldest existing cooperative in the city. Distinguished residents of this ten-story Queen Anne building have been *Yankee Doodle Dandy* James Cagney and Margaret Hamilton, widely known to American youngsters as the wicked witch in *The Wizard of Oz*. Facing directly on the park from the west stand five town houses dating from 1844 to 1850. Of special note to architectural buffs are the cast-iron porches of Nos. 3 and 4, with their traditional lamps. No. 4 was once the home of James Harper, mayor of New York City from 1844 to 1847.

Reflecting the tranquillity of another century, when landaus tied up at the gateposts and were guarded by what were then called "side boys," Gramercy Park is an historic district where the original beauty was so great that it has been able to resist the changes that could have destroyed it. Despite abortive attempts in 1890 and 1912 to run a trolley-car route through its verdant acres, Gramercy Park survives today as a graceful expression of another era.

Sniffen Court

DURING THE LATTER PART of the nineteenth century, when Manhattan's population hit one million, the Murray Hill district harbored many of New York's baroque mansions. Now most of these brownstones are gone, replaced by steel-and-glass skyscrapers like the Empire State Building, which opened its doors and 102 floors in 1931. But a group of stables that once belonged to the elegant families who lived in the leisurely magnificence of the surrounding streets can still be found in a narrow mews, saddled between Lexington and Third Avenues at 150-158 East 36th Street. This out-of-the-way oasis, called Sniffen Court, offers the visitor a glimpse into the back streets of J. Pierpont Morgan's New York as it must have looked more than one hundred fifty years ago.

John Sniffen constructed the carriage houses in the 1850s, about the same time William Marcy ("Boss") Tweed, the Tammany Hall leader, began his notorious climb to power. The court is comprised of ten brick structures designed in the early Romanesque Revival style. When the sound of hoofbeats and wagon wheels on cobblestones gave way to horseless carriages, the individual premises were converted into rustic residences. Over the past years many of them have undergone considerable change. The rounded arches, which originally served as the carriage entrances, have in some cases been filled in with bricks, while unusual window treatments have been installed in others. Yet, taken as a whole, there is a cohesive charm and tasteful tranquillity about Sniffen Court, which is now on the National Register of Historic Places and a distinct contrast to the race-track atmosphere on taxi-lined Lexington Avenue.

The battered bricks on the two gatehouses are painted dark chocolate and coach gray. Planters of well-groomed begonias and bottle-green boxwood brighten up the flagstone mews. Add to this picture such accessories as brass door knockers, lopsided lanterns, leaded-glass windows, and tangles of ivy, and you have a cul-de-sac that gives passing pedestrians a good reason to pull in their reins and peek through the formidable wrought-iron gate.

Today the stable that once reeked of oats and hay now smells of greasepaint, as it was converted into a small theater by the Sniffen Court Players. Its stage served as the starting gate for the career of accomplished actress Julie Harris. A longtime resident of the court is "Professor" Irwin Corey, actor and comedian, who performed on Broadway with actress Helen Hayes in *Mrs. McThing*. At the south end of the court, beyond a hand pump where Dobbin was once watered, stands the former studio of sculptress Malvina Hoffman, who decorated the wall with bas-relief plaques of Greek horsemen.

If you wish to drink in more of Murray Hill's history, then canter north to East 38th Street, where at No. 152 you'll find a charming neo-Federal town house set back in a luxuriant garden. It was constructed in 1858 as a carriage house for a member of President Martin Van Buren's family. In 1929 Cass Canfield, the publisher, purchased the place and in 1935 had it remodeled. Glancing across the street, your eyes fix upon a brick Dutch-gabled carriage house decorated with the heads of two ponies and a scrolled tablet over the door, attesting that it has stood there since 1902.

Beekman Place

"I ONLY REGRET that I have but one life to lose for my country." These were the last words spoken by twenty-one-year-old Nathan Hale, an American Revolutionary officer fresh out of Yale, before being hanged as a spy by the British in New York on September 22, 1776. This historic event took place in an orchard on the Beekman estate overlooking the East River, where today you find one of Manhattan's most distinguished enclaves, Beekman Place.

Beekman is an old New York family name. The founder of this Dutch dynasty, William Beekman, came to America with Peter Stuyvesant. He later became a burgomaster and acquired vast real estate holdings. In 1763, his heir, James Beekman, put up a large house on the property he purchased from John and Abraham Anderson. He called it Mount Pleasant. A pleasant place it was, furnished with delicately carved oaken chests, mahogany card tables, and oil paintings of his daughters by artist John Durand.

Everything at Mount Pleasant was in apple-pie order until the Revolutionary War broke out. Because of its strategic location by the river, British redcoats confiscated the estate and established headquarters there for their commanders, including General Howe. It was in the greenhouse behind the Beekman mansion that Nathan Hale, apprehended within enemy lines while seeking information, was first imprisoned and finally sentenced to death.

On Evacuation Day, James Beekman made a joyous return to his mansion and entertained American troops there. Afterward, the house stood for well over a century, until 1874, when it was razed to make room for the grid pattern of the city streets. The little community of commodious dwellings that sprang up on the site in the years that followed called itself Beekman Place in honor of the family that once resided there.

Toward the latter part of the nineteenth century, the neighborhood experienced an influx of impoverished immigrants. The area, dotted with discarded breweries and rotting warehouses, was completely forgotten until the early 1920s, when the river setting captured the imagination of a band of purposeful women, who were responsible for its return to polite society. Anne Morgan, Mrs. William K. Vanderbilt, and Elizabeth Marbury were those women. During those days of unlimited prosperity, it was their intention to build the two beautiful blocks running from Mitchell Place up to 51st Street that we know today as Beekman Place.

What makes this section of New York so special come rain or shine? Well, in addition to its connection with the Beekman family tree, the vistas from the backyards and balconies give considerable pleasure to the residents. Perched in penthouse gardens, they can observe gray-winged gulls swooping over tugboats chugging against the strong currents where the Harlem and East Rivers collide. The town houses, too, are something to see: eclectic rows of Georgian Colonial, French Renaissance, and English Tudor accentuated by gargoyles and porches under green copper roofs. To the south of Beekman Place rises the glass-walled United Nations Secretariat. By day a giant mirror, at night a glowing tower of light, it is indeed fitting that it should be located so close to the site where an early American patriot sacrificed his life so that millions could live in freedom.

Treadwell Farm

NOT FAR FROM THE BUSTLE of the great bazaar founded by Lyman and Joseph Bloomingdale in 1872, and a few blocks from the horse-drawn hansom cabs converging upon the Plaza Hotel, there is a friendly neighborhood of sycamore-shaded streets known as Treadwell Farm. Country bumpkins won't find chickens and ducks and geese scurrying here now, just row upon row of stylish town houses with shutters and doors painted in delicious shades of robin's-egg blue, burnt orange, and maize. Flower boxes of impatiens, geraniums, and ageratum bloom on every windowsill. But city slickers still insist upon calling the area Treadwell Farm because the houses were built on land that was once the working farm of Adam Treadwell.

Back in the early 1800s, Treadwell, a wealthy fur merchant, bought the property at public auction in the Tontine Coffee House from the heirs of Peter Van Zandt, who had owned the farm since colonial days. When Treadwell died in 1852, his prized property was divided equally among his heirs, who began to sell off their parcels to various buyers. Being civic-minded citizens, they reached an agreement with the purchasers, whereby standards for the height, width, and construction of the houses were set.

The happy result was that the residences now lining 61st and 62nd Streets between Third and Second Avenues were all built between 1868 and 1876 and are unique for their harmonious French Second Empire style of architecture. The fact that these rows have been so well maintained over the years makes them all the more remarkable for a city the size of New York.

By pounding these pavements today, you are following in the footsteps of the famous citizens who have called Treadwell Farm their home in the city: gifted writers like Paul Gallico and Clifton Fadiman; celebrities of stage and screen like Gertrude Lawrence and Montgomery Clift; and most distinguished of all, the great humanitarian and delegate to the United Nations, Eleanor Roosevelt.

If Treadwell Farm's bucolic atmosphere isn't enough to satisfy your appetite for country living in the city, then walk in the direction of the East River to the Mount Vernon Hotel Museum and Garden at 421 East 61st Street. Constructed of Manhattan schist as the carriage house for a country estate, the building was completed in 1799. When fire destroyed the main building in 1826, the carriage house was renovated and opened as the Mount Vernon Hotel. After the hotel closed, the house was owned privately until the twentieth century. In 1924, the Colonial Dames of America, a women's patriotic society, purchased the property. After extensive restoration, it was furnished with historic objects donated by its members. With nine richly appointed period rooms, it opened to the public in 1939. The lovely eighteenth-century gardens surrounding the building with espaliers of ivy climbing on trellised walls offer a peaceful respite from the bumper-to-bumper traffic on FDR Drive. Just a block south the lacy-structured Queensborough Bridge, designed by Gustav Lindenthal and opened in 1909, begins its graceful rise over the East River. A stroll beneath its Catalan vaults and through the newly opened bridge marketplace affords you the opportunity to appreciate the marvelous tile work created and installed by Rafael Guastavino.

Henderson Place

HEAD EAST ON 86TH STREET, through the heart of jovial Yorkville and between York and East End Avenues, and you come upon Henderson Place, two dozen diminutive dwellings holding their own against a mountainous apartment house that overshadows them. With their parapets, gables, and chimney pots, these Rumpelstiltskin-style residences stand today as a small reminder of Yorkville's quiet domestic charm back in the nineteenth century, when beer barons such as Jacob Ruppert had their manor houses here.

The area was settled in the 1790s by German immigrants who named it Yorkville to emphasize that it was a part of New York. In the early 1830s, the country road leading from the Hell Gate ferry landing was graded and made an important east-west thoroughfare, which we now know as 86th Street. At about the same time the New York and Harlem Railroad laid tracks up from the city. This put the village within easy traveling distance, and many leading German families—the Ruppert, the Ringlings, and the Rhine-landers, to name a few—built their homes in the area. The Ruppert Brewery, a feudal fortress of belching smokestacks and rattling beer barrels, was a landmark that could be seen, heard, and smelled for miles around.

Today, getting to Henderson Place is half the fun. As you hike on across 86th Street, you are caught up in an Oktoberfest of taverns, delis, and shops. Around the corner on Second Avenue, Schaller & Weber's windows display a bevy of beer steins, one featuring "Red Baron" Von Richtofhen, World War I German flying ace, and Tyrolean nutcrackers, all standing at attention beneath strings of smoked bratwurst, knock-wurst, and beerwurst sausages.

Next door, at the Heidelberg Restaurant, billed as "Manhattan's favorite German beer garden" since 1939, you are given a *Willkommen* as you grab a stool at the oaken bar covered by a trellis entwined with twinkling lights. First off, order a frosty mug of Dinkelacker on draft. Then take a table and order Wiener Schnitzel a la Holstein, a breaded veal cutlet topped with fried egg, anchovies, and capers.

Farther down at 1628 Second Avenue, the Elk Candy Company, established in 1933, lures you like a Lorelei with handmade continental chocolates and nonpareils. Mouthwatering mounds of marzipan made of almond paste and sugar shaped like potatoes, pigs, and ladybugs tantalize your tastebuds.

Leaving the lederhosen and liebfraumilch behind, you arrive at Henderson Place, a cul-de-sac hibernating near Carl Schurz Park. Of the original thirty-two Queen Anne dwellings built in 1882 by John C. Henderson for "persons of moderate means," only twenty-four remain wrapped around the corner onto East End Avenue. Now the block has been declared an historic district, which most certainly pleased former Mayor Rudy Guiliani, because during his term in office he lived just across the street in Gracie Mansion. This white-frame house with Georgian verandas and Chinese Chippen-dale railings was built by the Scottish shipping tycoon Archibald Gracie in 1799. For a closer look at Gracie Mansion, which lies on Horn's Hook, take the John Finley Walk, a metal-railed promenade lined with benches and sandboxes above the East River, where barge traffic salutes the little lighthouse at the tip of Roosevelt Island.

Strawberry Fields

DESPITE ITS 840 ACRES, New York's Central Park, by a stretch of the imagination, can be considered an enclave. Surrounded by residential towers on four sides—Fifth Avenue to Central Park West, 59th Street to 110th Street—the greensward that took designers Frederick Law Olmstead and Calvert Vaux twenty years to complete serves as an arboretum inside a vast metropolis. Within this scenic landmark of sweeping lawns, rambles, and bridle paths is an enclave with a certain poignant history. It is Strawberry Fields, just 3½ acres of uncommon greenery, a serene, rolling landscape dedicated to the memory of John Lennon, the quintessential musician. In February 1964, four youngsters from Liverpool who called themselves the Beatles landed in New York City and were greeted by five thousand adoring fans. On the following Sunday, John Lennon, Paul McCartney, George Harrison, and Ringo Starr appeared on the *Ed Sullivan Show* before a record-breaking television audience of seventy-three million. Overnight America was besotted with Beatlemania. In the years that followed, the Beatles performed and recorded hit after hit: "Strawberry Fields Forever" in 1967, "Hey Jude" in 1968, and "Let It Be" in 1970, their final single before splitting up. After the breakup of the Beatles, John Lennon and his wife, Japanese avant-garde artist Yoko Ono, moved into the Dakota Apartment House on Central Park West. Lennon enjoyed the fortresslike building's turrets, towers, chimneys, and brewery-brick Victorian facade. Built in 1884 by Edward S. Clark, heir to the Singer sewing machine fortune, he named it in response to a friend's remark that West 72nd Street was in Native-American territory: "Why don't you go a few blocks more and build it out in Dakota?"

Leaving the Dakota and heading across Central Park West to its entrance just north of West 72nd Street, you enter Strawberry Fields. The dream of Yoko Ono Lennon, it was her generous donation that provided for the creation and upkeep of this "Garden of Peace" in memory of the legendary Beatle. Gazing about, you can take in more than 121 species of plants and trees, all representing the countries of the United Nations.

You may then join visitors from every corner of the globe as they gather at the black-and-gray-tile mosaic impressed in the pavement with the word IMAGINE at its center, a gift from Naples, Italy, and a homage to Lennon's most successful album. On the velvet lawns and the memorial benches surrounding the shrine, people hold hands, light votive candles, leave messages, and lay fresh flowers as they reminisce about the glory days of the Fab Four. Wandering farther on toward a tall pin oak tree, your eye is caught by a brass plaque affixed to a rock outcropping on the right. It bears the words written by John Lennon: "Imagine all the people living in Peace."

After exploring Strawberry Fields, several whimsical side trips remain on your Central Park agenda. These include visits to the pond at the Loeb Boathouse, the Friedman Memorial Merry-Go-Round, and the Tavern on the Green at West 67th Street, a culinary landmark that began as a sheepfold in 1870. Now, at long last, lift a flute of champagne and drink a toast to John Lennon (1940–1980), for his imaginative music, and to love, peace, and understanding. ✐

Strivers' Row

To walk west from Adam Clayton Powell Jr. Boulevard along West 138th and West 139th Streets is to step abruptly into a mellow remnant of the 1890s. For here, nestled beneath the Gothic tower of the City College of New York, is a rare jewel in Manhattan's diminishing store of architectural treasures: the houses of Strivers' Row in Harlem's St. Nicholas historic district. These three rows of distinguished town houses, one in Georgian Revival, the other two in Italian Renaissance style, were constructed in 1891 by David H. King, who was also responsible for the base of the Statue of Liberty.

When Harlem was founded by the Dutch in 1636, it was called Nieu Haarlem, after the town in the Netherlands. By 1820, the rural outpost had only ninety-one families, one church, one school, and one library. Still a village, it was dominated by the estates of wealthy farmers known as patroons. During the Civil War, Harlem went into a temporary decline. Many of the large estates were auctioned off because of worn-out soil. This included Alexander Hamilton's Grange, designed by John McComb, Jr., in 1801. The house, however, stubbornly stands today, crowded behind a church at 287 Convent Avenue near 141st Street, one of the few country seats of the Federal period remaining in New York.

In 1878, when the elevated railroad was extended to 129th Street, Harlem became a commuting point from downtown. By the mid 1880s, the area was converted into one of the city's most fashionable neighborhoods. Rows of elegant homes sprang up, with wrought-iron balconies out front and carriage houses in back. Gate number 6 on 138th Street still carries the message: "Private Road. Walk Your Horses."

African Americans have always lived in Harlem, first as slaves in the seventeenth century and then as farmers or domestic servants following emancipation. Around the turn of the twentieth century came the collapse of the Harlem land boom, and a great number of African Americans moved from downtown.

Today the beige and russet-brown town houses of Strivers' Row, one block designed by Stanford White, are occupied by many African-American ministers, merchants, physicians, and college professors. Notable residents over the years have been Eubie Blake, composer of "I'm Just Wild About Harry" (221 West 139th), and W. C. Handy, who wrote "St. Louis Blues" (232 West 139th).

In the 1920s and 1930s, Harlem was a place for a night's prowl. It meant cellar cabarets, where jazz singer Ethel Waters warbled "Harlem on My Mind." It promised the Apollo Theater on 125th Street, where Louis "Satchmo" Armstrong tooted his sweet trumpet and "Lady Day" Billie Holiday sang the blues with a gardenia behind her ear. It beckoned one to the Cotton Club, where Duke Ellington's bandsmen let loose with "Take the A Train."

Now, at the turn of the twenty-first century, Harlem is much more than this. It is a thriving community of businesses, schools, churches, homes, shops, and entertainments. So, after strolling along the shady streets of Strivers' Row and savoring the shops on 125th Street, saunter over to Sylvia's Restaurant at 3128 Lenox Avenue. Here the Queen of Soul Food serves up such delicacies as pork chitterlings with collard greens and her world-famous, talked-about barbecue ribs. Sylvia's southern hospitality has been a happy tradition in historic Harlem since 1962.

Jumel Terrace

HIGH ON A HILL overlooking the Harlem River, a number of town houses cluster about a Georgian mansion like chicks around a mother hen. This quiet little village-within-a-city, located just off St. Nicholas Avenue near 160th Street, is known as the Jumel Terrace historic district. By far the best approach is to climb the steps that lead from the avenue up to a tiny street called Sylvan Terrace. Here you are greeted by two rows of charming little houses that seem about to tumble down the hill. Built in 1882, these dollhouse-like dwellings beguile the eye. When you reach the crest of the hill, you are afforded a sweeping view of one of the city's great masterpieces, the Morris-Jumel mansion, a house filled with history.

If buildings could talk, this clapboard and shingle abode, with a grand Tuscan portico supported by a two-story Doric colonnade and crowned with a captain's walk, would have some story to tell. In 1765 Colonel Roger Morris, a loyal Tory, bought the hundred-acre farm from James Carroll, a butcher. Morris built his country house on the property that very same year. The Morrises lived there until the beginning of hostilities in 1775, when they fled to England. After the battle of Long Island, Washington retreated to Mount Morris and made the mansion his headquarters from September 14 to October 18, 1776. It was here that the battle of Harlem Heights was fought, during which the Continental army won its first victory.

By 1790, when Washington returned to the house where he visited with Thomas Jefferson, John Adams, John Quincy Adams, and Alexander Hamilton, it had been turned into a tavern called Calumet Hall for travelers heading northward. The mansion was purchased for ten thousand dollars by Stephen Jumel, a successful wine merchant. The old manor house was fast falling into decay when his wife, Eliza, oversaw a glittering restoration in the Second Empire style. When the flamboyant redhead completed the interior decorating, the mansion was reputed to be one of the most sumptuous in the country.

The year after Jumel's death in 1832, his rich fifty-eight-year-old widow married Aaron Burr, the seventy-seven-year-old fortune hunter and former vice president under Thomas Jefferson. This tumultuous marriage was of short duration and ended in divorce. Still, Madame Jumel lived in the mansion with a retinue of servants until her death in 1865 at the ripe old age of ninety-three. It was purchased by the Department of Parks in 1905 and opened to the public as a museum.

Today, the octagonal drawing room, where General Washington plotted military strategy, and the other rooms of this house-museum are furnished with some of the personal belongings of Madame Jumel. Items include her bed, which is thought to have once belonged to Napoleon, and an antique writing desk used by Aaron Burr. A visit here and a walk through the gardens and surrounding streets take you back to the days when Manhattan was dotted with sprawling country estates connected by curving carriage drives. Most of them are gone with the wind, but the Morris-Jumel mansion still stubbornly stands, a bit the worse for wear, and receives about fifteen thousand visitors a year. No house in America has been inhabited or visited by a greater array of Revolutionary War statesmen than the gracious mansion perched atop the hill in the delightful Jumel Terrace historic district. ✍♥

Dyckman Farm House Park

MORE THAN THREE HUNDRED YEARS AGO Manhattan Island, from Peter Stuyvesant's Bouwerie up to Spuyten Duyvil, snoozed under a patchwork quilt of orchards, tobacco fields, and vegetable gardens. This bucolic scene has been plowed under, replaced today by rows of apartment houses and macadam roads teeming with traffic. Despite these drastic changes, there is one lone survivor of the sleepy-time days when New York was simply a gently rolling countryside. This is Dyckman Farm House Park, where the last Dutch American farmhouse left in Manhattan still stands.

The story of this small enclave began in 1661, when Jan Dyckman, a native of Bentheim, Westphalia, came to America and purchased several acres near Spuyten Duyvil from Simon de Ruine. Dyckman was a good farmer, and with the help of his wife, Rebecca, the farm prospered. When Dyckman died in 1715, his son, Jacob, and his grandson, William, expanded the property to three hundred acres. During the Revolutionary War, the peaceful existence of the farm was broken by battling armies, which took turns occupying the land. First Washington's troops camped here. Then the area became the site of the Hessian hut camp, consisting of some fifty log cabins. When the British deserted the farm, they destroyed the house and orchards. Following the war in 1784, William Dyckman resolutely set about rebuilding a dwelling with strong Dutch influences near the site of the original homestead. Salvaging some materials from the original, he constructed the house with hand-hewn stud rivet laths held together with homemade nails and fillings of mud and marsh grass. When he died in 1787, Jacobus Dyckman, a grad-uate of Columbia College, took over. He later bequeathed the property to Isaac and Michael Dyckman. In 1871, the farm passed from the family, but in 1915 it was purchased and presented to the City of New York as the Dyckman Farm House Park and Museum by Mary Alice Dyckman Dean and Fannie Fredericka Welch Dyckman in memory of their parents, Isaac and Fannie Dyckman.

Today, the modest one-and-a-half-story field-stone farmhouse, with its charming front porch facing out from beneath a gambrel roof, sits on what little land is left of the original three hundred-acre farm on Broadway at West 204th Street in the Inwood section of the city. Walking through its double doors, one enters the home of a wealthy farmer from 1810. In the parlor, a portrait of Jacob Dyckman hangs near an original mantelpiece, and a big Dutch Bible that belonged to William waits to be read. Dominating the dining room with its random-width chestnut floors is a fireplace decorated with Delft tiles. Upstairs awaiting your inspection is a period bedroom complete with cradle, commode, and a high four-poster bedstead. Down a crooked staircase one lands in an early American kitchen, warmed by a cozy fireplace.

In the garden behind the farmhouse and the attached bakehouse stand the smokehouse, the old Dyckman well, and a little Hessian hut. Reconstructed with materials found in the British officers' dugout camp, the hut is one of the few structures left to remind us that the British army occupied New York City during the American Revolution. What's more, the bakehouse, circa 1725, just might be the very oldest wooden building left on Manhattan Island.

Acknowledgments

This book would not have been complete without the resources gathered from a host of New York City entities. These include the New York Public Library's History and Genealogy Division, the New York Landmarks Preservation Commission, the American Institute of Architects, New York Chapter, the New-York Historical Society, the Museum of the City of New York, the *New York Times*, the New York Convention and Visitors Bureau, the Sons of the Revolution of the State of New York, the South Street Seaport Museum, the Friends of Cast Iron Architecture, the Washington Square Outdoor Art Exhibit, the Morris-Jumel Museum, and the Dyckman Farm House Park and Museum.

I am indeed indebted to all the people in the neighborhoods scattered about Manhattan Island who told me what they knew and loved about their own particular enclave: from the haberdashers on Orchard Street and the merchants in Chinatown to the benchwarmers in Washington Square; from the cops on the beat on Stuyvesant Street and the doormen in Gramercy Park to the butchers in Yorkville and the strollers in Central Park.

I also want to express my appreciation to Elizabeth Royles, my editor, whose contagious enthusiasm for my 1975 book made this new and updated edition in 2003 happen. Also, to Annetta Hanna and Melissa Bustos, my sincere thanks for seeing it through to completion.

My writer's hat is off to Marie Huebner, whose crackerjack computer produced the finished manuscript despite the demanding author's many changes and additions. What's more, I appreciate the support given by Jane Allison of the Point Lookout Library. My sons Bill, Brendan, Joey, and Christopher provided encouragement from a distance, for which I am grateful.

Last, but most certainly not least, I want to thank my wife, Maggie, and my sister, Betty, for urging me year after year to contact my publisher in an attempt to have the drawings and detailed descriptions of the enclaves be seen, read, and enjoyed by a new generation of New Yorkers as well as visitors to Manhattan Island.

About the Author

William H. Hemp is the author-artist of three books, including *New York Enclaves*, *If Ever You Go to Dublin Town*, and *Taos: Landmarks & Legends*. He served as a television talk-show host in Taos, New Mexico, and lives on Long Island, New York, near the ocean with his wife, Maggie.